Maryse Noël Roumain, Ph.D.

EVOCATIONS OF MY PAST

SKETCHES OF A HAITIAN WOMAN'S LIFE

Order this book online at www.trafford.com
or email orders@trafford.com

Most Trafford titles are also available at major online book retailers.

Printed in the United States of America.

ISBN: 978-1-4269-7082-5 (sc)
ISBN: 978-1-4269-7083-2 (e)

Trafford rev. 06/15/2011

 www.trafford.com

North America & international
toll-free: 1 888 232 4444 (USA & Canada)
phone: 250 383 6864 ♦ fax: 812 355 4082

Foreword

Seize chapitres d'une vie déjà marquée, dès l'enfance, par l'annonce d'un destin singulier dans et hors d'un pays, Haïti, dont le grand écrivain, anthropologue et homme politique Anténor Firmin (1850-1911) a dit qu'il était un « singulier petit pays.»

This book presents sixteen chapters that evoke my mother's personal stamp on our lives and her desire for her girls to be the best they can be... the profound love for a self-effaced father, a man of modest ambitions, as well as the bullies who forced me into isolation and loneliness ...my best friend who rescued me but fell prey to the boogey man, the tonton macoute, a high profile ideologue of the Duvalier regime...my provincial hometown by the Caribbean sea... how the voodoo cult nourished my fears but delighted my passion for dance and music...my fist love...

You may say this is an unfinished book and you will be right. Whether or not I complete it depends on the circumstances of my life. In the meantime, I hope you share the interest in reading the beginning of my story...

"A person is a fluid process...a flowing river of change...a continually changing constellation of potentialities"

(Carl Rogers, On Becoming a Person)

1

In God, I Trusted -1

It wasn't a communion like any other. It was a "private" event orchestrated by my mother. The year before, my classmates had their first communion, but I was only six then and my mother had found me too young to make this important allegiance to God. It was to happen when I was 7, the age of reason. So she taught me the catechism and took me to the priest the following year.

I passed the test with high marks; my mother was a good teacher and the stories of the old and new testaments had captivated my emotions and imagination.

On the day of this important event, I was wearing a white embroidered dress, a white hat; I was holding a white purse; my small feet were inserted in white socks and white shoes. In my left hand was what must have probably been a small bible. "You look very pretty", said my mom as I was feeling taken by the sentiment of the uniqueness of the day.

We woke up early to get prepared to go to the cathedral. There was a lot of excitement and a feeling this day would be like no other, an exceptional one in my life. The day before I had gone to the hairdresser, for the first time, to get my hair straightened and curled with a hot comb. I remember the scent of talcum powder while passing through my mom's bedroom that morning on my way to the living room where my attire was carefully arranged and displayed on one of the mahogany chairs.

At the church, I walked alone in the aisle… among adults it seems.

What I recall most about this period of my childhood is that I was the youngest in the class and skinny to the bone. My classmates were one or two years older than me. I was smarter than them. I was very verbal, using both Creole and French; school tasks seemed easy and I enjoyed learning. None of them became my friend. I yearned to one day have one who would love me unconditionally, whom I could confide in and who would keep me company. We would have an exclusive rapport, a one-on-one camaraderie that would last forever and never be betrayed.

I wasn't the only child of my parents. We were seven children, six girls and one boy and I had a brother and a sister from my father's side before he married my mother. Between my older brother and me, there was a difference of five years and between me and my younger sister, another difference of five years. She was 2 when I was seven; she could not possibly have been my friend when I was growing up. As for my brother, besides the age difference, he normally preferred the company of young males.

I sometimes felt like an only child.

Through the role she played in my first communion, my mother expressed the desire, the will, to have her say in my upbringing. She would not passively accept what the school dictated; she knew better and was ready to intervene. My mother was instrumental in selecting the schools we attended, our religious orientation; she influenced and supported our vocational preferences, and whether we played guitar, piano, took dance lessons or participated in theatrical performances. My mother did not believe in passivity, but in voluntarism. She was the opposite of my father who was an accepting person, non-adventurous and unwilling to take risks. My father was easily intimidated and fearful; my mother had a strong character and was forceful. His ambitions for us, especially the girls, were moderate; my mother wanted us to achieve our greatest potential. "My advice to you", he told my mother, "is that the girls

2

should go make a living at the fabric store, after they complete their 9th grade". My mother's ambition was for her first daughter to attend Medical School. And she did.

My father played an active role in our education however. After all, he was an educator. He believed in raising children who received the preparation and enlightenment the schools provide. He is the one who helped us with homework, most of the time anyway. I remember the blackboard in the dining room downstairs where we learned spelling and arithmetic. I was good at spelling and enjoyed putting together difficult words. Father had an easy job with me.

My father was not politically oriented. He was not a member of a political party and refrained from participating in the voting process or even having a preferred candidate. In matters of politics, he was rather pessimistic and keenly aware of the dangers involved.

He was not a church devout like my mother. While he respected my mother's religious beliefs, he never went to church himself. He was, above all, a skeptic.

Both my father and mother were the breadwinners, they both provided for us: my father as a rural educator and administrator, my mother as a teacher first and then a store keeper. He worked for the public schools in the provinces and the countryside. Deceived by the public teachers' low paycheck, she held what was once a successful commerce. I used to spend time in the 'boutique' with her, studying, observing her interactions with the people who came to buy her products. That is where I hid at carnival times when young men dressed as "werewolves" took the streets to scare away little children who could not make the difference between the masks and the real person. I used to be scared to death at carnival times; I needed to stay close to my mother.

2

In God, I Trusted -2

There were other people in my life. The servants, adults and children, played a major role. They cooked, did house chores, went to the market for food, washed and ironed our clothes. My grandmother always made sure the children were my age so they could play with me. While my mother had no hesitation about laying them off and replacing them for one reason or another, I longed they could stay forever and not have to develop new relations with new people. They knew our folklore and told us tales at night as well as guessing riddles in Haitian Creole. We sat in the dining room lighted by a kerosene lamp. There was no electricity. They did not speak French. We did. They did not know how to read or write. We did.

The conscience of the precariousness of servant life is my first awareness of social class differences. Spontaneously I understood the plight of the poor and the oppressed. I did not agree with their condition. The reprobation was obvious in my eyes, my silence. My mother did not like the fact that I was not always on her side. "You're taking the servants' side", she said to me, with disapprobation in her eyes.

On the other hand I could understand that we were not rich. Although my family owned a house, was able to procure us with basic food and clothing, send some of us to private school in the capital city Port-au-Prince, there were others who had more means. "We were not poor, we were not rich", my mother says.

My social awareness also included the consciousness of upper classes. We did not live in the same neighborhood nor go to the same church. Ours was the Sacred Heart across from the open market; theirs was the Cathedral across from the public square on the upper side of the town. We lived in wood houses; they lived in concrete houses that were bigger. My mother had a struggling commerce; they had big stores and businesses. They sold fabrics or imported products, exported coffee and the vetiver grass which was used abroad to make expensive perfume.

As for God, my relation with him was a serious one: I loved him with all my heart and believed in him; in return, he would protect me. It was a mutual understanding, a two-way pact never to be broken. My commitment to God was conditional. He was all powerful and would take me under his wings, secure me from harm and the death of my loved ones. I was a fragile child who needed to feel safe and that's the way I could figure out my relationship with God. He was my protector in heaven. In return, I would be a good girl and would commit no sin.

I was a very energetic little girl who needed to always be occupied in a lot of activities to pass time, so I became a girl scout, participated in dance and theater, and organized theatrical performances for the neighbors. During the summer, I would go to the countryside where I enjoyed bathing at the river as well as eating the mangoes, the sugar cane, the coconut fruit, the corn beverage and other typical goodies as well as spend time with my cousins. I remember my aunt Therese. She was married to my uncle Eng. She had a granddaughter who came from the capital city Port-au-Prince for the summer who needed company. I was smart and I spoke French so she always sent for me to come and stay with her granddaughter in the village of Cavaillon where my mother was born and had family roots. I spent several summers there.

3

Of Good and Evil -1

The voodoo priest is sometimes referred to as *Doktè Fèy (herb Doctor)* because of his use of the traditional herbal medicine but voodoo played no important part in our household. One of the town doctors was a friend of the family (How lucky we were!) He was born in the village of Saint Louis du Sud where my father originated. He is the one who was called when we were sick. He did not charge my parents for his service. When a physician was not available, a midwife helped deliver my mother's babies, like in my case she tells me.

Periodically, we took a purgative, a beverage, made with leaves, that was so bitter we had to eat an orange after drinking it. This was to prevent us from having worms and to cleanse our body. At the time, we were vaccinated in school against some of the childhood illnesses and a mixture of starch was used to help us with diseases such as measles…

So, my mother did not resort to the hougan or mambo, voodoo priest or priestess, when her business declined. She was not involved in the sorcery aspects of voodoo and never went to the *"bòkòr"* or sorcerer. She did not go to them for protection, or to become rich nor for any other reason people seek their help or know-how for. She kept her distance and honored God only.

I remember however that she, once a year, made private offerings to the *"marasa loas"* when she dressed a small table in the corner of our bedroom with mints, peanuts, cola and other candies which we could not touch or eat since it was for the loas, the voodoo spirits:

"You are forbidden to eat or even touch this or something bad will happen to you", said my mom.

Marasa is Haitian Creole for twins. My grandmother was a twin and the twins were considered to have special powers. The *Marasa Loas* are the sacred twins of voodoo. They represent abundance, blessings, the gift of children, the sacredness of the family and the mysteries of the divine. They are, I read, most commonly identified with the twin saints Cosmos and Damien.

We, the children, were kept away from this activity and the meaning of all this. Offering sweets to the *marasa loas* was part of my mother's cultural and religious heritage; she did not want to share it with us. This ritual was, I guess, so her business could prosper and so she could always have the means to provide for us.

Magical primitive beliefs were present in the *ordalies* performed by my aunt Ava to determine who stole my mother's jewelry or money. She would have us and especially the servants stand in a circle and dramatically invoked St Peter and St Paul to reveal who was the thief: "By St Peter or St Paul, I shall know the truth", said my aunt Ava with a loud voice. That was an impressive ceremony by which God rendered his judgment. This practice is different from voodoo however since in the last the hougan or voodoo priest would have used his powers of divinity to determine the guilty, but it is also a primitive procedure rooted in ancient beliefs.

4

Of Good and Evil -2

To this day I remain estranged to the practice of voodoo never having attended a ceremony or consulted a voodoo priest or priestess. When I got sick, I turned to the doctor, the psychotherapist, I invoked God. When I wanted to get money, I looked for a job. When I wanted to influence the course of history, I turned to political activism. When I went abroad, I never felt the urge to go back to my voodoo roots in Haiti and make offerings, organize a ceremony for the spirits to beg for their forgiveness. When I encountered misfortune, I did not attribute it to the powers of voodoo.

I feel however that given the importance of this cult or religion if you will, in our society, I should not be so distant or ignorant. So when I grew up, I read some books on voodoo and God, voodoo and theater, voodoo and psychiatry, the anti-voodoo campaign under the American occupation and so on.

The voodooists believe in God and Catholicism not just in the spirits. It's a syncretistic religion and not a superstition as the Haitian writer and anthropologist Jacques Roumain, the author of Masters of the Dew, wrote. I know at least that much, but on this matter, I must admit it, I remain an outsider. (1)

So was our world: religious, magical and mystical. And, within it, people like us who tried to sort things out and understand. As a child, I was kept away and stayed away from what I assimilated to also be the domain of secret societies of evildoers, werewolves, poisoning, zombies, animal sacrifices, human persecution, cannibalism and cataleptic trance or possession by the spirit. I was completely alienated from this estranged world.

At night time, I heard the drums from a distance; I observed from afar the *"rara"* bands passing by.

I remain however an unconditional fanatic of voodoo rhythms, dances and music. And the artistic part of voodoo is so much in my blood it must have been acquired at an early age. I believe voodoo to be an intrinsic part of our culture and to influence us in one way or another whether we like it or not. It is part of who we are as a people and an individual- although not to the same degree for everyone.

Voodoo also answers to our spiritual aspirations and needs for a world beyond, a God who is bigger than us and can protect us and can accompany us in times of trouble and difficulty. All children, including those who come from the voodoo circles, need God in their lives. The world is too big, immense and incomprehensible to little children; there is too much that they don't know, they feel too insecure and unsafe, they are too lonely and need too much to be reassured. The "presence" of God is to them comforting and securing so they rely on him, the Almighty.

(1)
Here is the quotation by Jacques Roumain:

"Is Voodoo a superstition?
…Voodoo represents a catholic-voodoo syncretism expressing a distinctive religious conception of the world…It is more a question of superposition, of a symbiosis. It's a phenomenon that the works of Drs. Price-Mars, J.C. Dorsainvil, Professor Melville, J. Herskovits have studied and explained…"
(A Propos de la Campagne Antisuperstitieuse, Œuvres Complètes, pp.745-752)

5

My Native Town, Les Cayes, The Land along the Edge of the Sea

My native town 'Aux Cayes' which has been renamed 'Les Cayes' is located southwest of the Capital, Port-au-Prince. The name comes from the French quay or in English shore, meaning a land along the edge of the sea.

Les Cayes is the third most important town after Port-au-Prince in the West and Cap-Haïtien in the north. It is a city, or better a province, the chef-lieu of six municipalities or villages considered to be rural and rustic, referred to as 'La campagne' (the country side in English) or in Haitian Creole 'andéyò', 'nan mòn', meaning those mountainous regions that are on the outskirts of the city and are inhabited by the peasants, pejoratively referred to as unrefined and lacking in good manners and urban sophistication.

Our town borders the Caribbean Sea and has port facilities, exporting coffee, sugar cane and other agricultural products abroad. It's built in the Plaine des Cayes, is thus flat and easily flooded when the river, the Ravine du Sud, would overflow during the hurricane season, carrying muddy waters and rocks that invaded in the streets and homes. And so it suffered from the winds and fury of several violent storms and hurricanes such as Hazel in October 1954, Flora in October 1963, Cleo in August 1964 and others.

I remember my uncle T, who lived by the ocean, coming to take refuge at our home which was on the other side of town and thus better protected from the flooding waters. In the eighteen century, during the colonial period, two hurricanes destroyed the town which was later rebuilt.

There were public, Catholic and private schools up to the secondary level, two big Catholic churches, two police stations, a public square, a public market, government administration houses, an army barrack with military personnel, big and small stores...

The town had its poor, its middle class and its bourgeois class. It had its Middle Eastern community coming from Syria, Lebanon, Palestine, all referred to as Syrians. They came with nothing but soon ended up selling fabric by the public market and mostly marrying each other exclusively. The province had its Monsignor. When I was a child it was a Monsignor who came from Quebec so he spoke French; later, when Papa Doc Duvalier nationalized the church, it was a Haitian bishop. He resided in a big solid house by the cathedral near the public square.

It took a whole day by truck or van to go from Aux Cayes to Port-au-Prince only 196 kilometers away. Then, the roads were not covered with asphalt. They were rocky and muddy when it rained and the van could get stuck for several hours. Everybody would come out then and the men would push it out of the deep and large potholes. There were mountainous roads to pass through. Haiti is an Indian word for mountainous land and as the proverb say: *dèyè mòn gen mòn*, behind mountains there are mountains. In the vehicle, the passengers sat in close proximity to each other; on top of it were the goods brought to the capital city's market including the live poultry that was for long hours exposed to the sun.

I sometimes accompanied my mother who went to the capital city to buy products for her commerce.

Aux Cayes had its beaches, the most famous being "Gelée", where the river met with the ocean and Boury sur Mer, to the south. The town had its waterfall called La Perle or the Pearl; its vacation places where a privileged few owned second homes in Camp-Perrin and Pont Salomon. It had its Patron Saint Our Lady of Assumption celebrated on the fifteenth of August.

6

Les Cayes: Political History

My hometown, Les Cayes, had its political history too and its natives who became presidents and otherwise famous.

Of the history of Les Cayes, I retain the passage of Simon Bolivar who, eleven years after Haiti's independence, came to gather arms and munitions to free the countries of South America. There is a bust of him on the seaport of our hometown. We passed it every time we went to the boardwalk for a promenade. The hero of South American independence, supplied by the then president of Haiti, Alexandre Pétion, sailed two times from our coastal town to successfully conclude his struggle for freedom from Spanish colonialism.

We were proud of the peasants who dared to protest at a near location called Marchaterre against the American occupation which occurred from 1915 to 1934. There used to be a cross standing there to recall and honor their memories.

Of the presidents, there were Nicolas Geffrard, and Antoine Simon (among others) who came from the region although the last was turned into ridicule because of his simple mindedness and lack of education.

The African American woman writer Zora Neale Hurston tells the story of Antoine Simon. She writes there are countless tales of this crude soldier's stumbling and blunders in the palace where most considered he had no right to be; his not knowing what to do in matters of state, what to say to foreign diplomats and how to behave among the luxuries of the palace. "Some politicians engineered General Simon, then the governor of the South, to the presidency, hoping to manipulate him. What they had to reckon with instead was his daughter Celestine, a voodoo priestess, and his mystical pet, the goat Simalo... There are tales of the services to the voodoo spirits when his army marched from Aux Cayes to Port-au-Prince; especially the ceremonies to Ogoun Feray, the voodoo god of war, to make the soldiers impervious to bullet and blade."

When Antoine Simon and his daughter Celestine came to power, Hurston writes, voodoo ceremonies were regularly held at the basement chambers of the palace causing fear among upper class Haitians.

Antoine Simon remained president for three years. He was like many other presidents exiled to Jamaica when President Cincinatus Leconte overthrew and replaced him in 1911 prior to the American occupation.

The more recent political figure of which Aux Cayes was most proud of is Louis Déjoie, a presidential candidate in 1956-1957 against Francois Duvalier, Clément Jumelle and Daniel Fignolé.

I was 8 years old when these historical events unfolded having been born in 1949. This election was to be the first one by universal suffrage so everyone had their say. (Prior to that, the chambers nominated the president or he seized power at the head of his army). It was also the first where women, who had obtained the right to vote in 1950, were participating.

During the electoral campaign, mass meetings were held mostly by the candidate Déjoie who visited Aux Cayes coming from Port-au-Prince where he resided. I attended one of them perched on the shoulders of my uncle T. Every one wore straw hats which said: Vive Déjoie or Long Life to Déjoie!

He was a rich landowner and industrialist who promised to give the people work if he was elected: *voter Déjoie, c'est voter travail*, to vote for Déjoie is to vote for work, said his slogan. He was a mulatto and had the support of most of the bourgeoisie but also of the middle class and the peasants in aux Cayes and its surrounding region where he owned and cultivated land.

The army was on the side of Duvalier and that's how he got to win through fraudulent, manipulated elections.

According to my father, we should stay away from politics because in Haiti it is dangerous and treacherous but my oldest sister who just turned twenty one and attended medical school in Port-au-Prince wanted to participate. She was all excited and proud. Women, for the first time, were exercising their right to vote. I remember her, coming back from the voting poll, and proudly showing her finger wet with red ink so she could not vote again.

After Duvalier won the election, there was a price to pay for having been on the side of Déjoie. And so the richer families, especially, were constantly ransomed and harassed; their daughters became the sexual prey of the tontons macoutes. This historical epoch is best described in Raoul Peck's movie: 'The Man by the Shore' which in fact depicts the story of my godmother, her daughter and grand children in Aux Cayes, after Duvalier became president.

As I recall it, my godmother's daughter had married an army officer who was on the side of the candidate Déjoie. He was forced to flee into exile when Duvalier was elected leaving behind his wife, his three daughters and his mother-in-law (my godmother) to look after them. The movie tells the story as seen in the eyes of the youngest granddaughter of their stay in Aux Cayes where they waited until they were rejoined with their mother and father abroad. The kids were more or less my age and I used to go spend time with them in the big concrete house with an attic and a piano. The wife was filled with grief and sadness. This episode caused my godmother a lot of political persecution.

After that period, we never saw elections again since Duvalier proclaimed himself president for life and his nineteen year old son succeeded him, both of them ruling for close to thirty years. It was the reign of the tontons macoutes, or boogey men, as the new militia was called.

Many voodoo worshipers entered the Tontons Macoutes, and Duvalier installed a psychosis of fear through superstitious beliefs. The flag became again black and red rather than blue and red with a guinea hen in its middle for an emblem rather than the arms of the republic; and every morning in school we stood in ranks singing the national anthem and swearing to be the guardians of the "revolution".

At Port-au-Prince, my oldest sister went to school at first at the most prestigious Catholic school Ste Rose de Lima, then at the public medical school or Faculté de Médecine. She stayed at her godmother's, the Edlines, a mulatto family who originated from Aux Cayes. They were not rich mulattoes, rather middle class. The father was a mechanic. I used to stay at their place when my mother came to the capital. One of the daughters had married a black military officer Francois Benoît who also originated from Aux Cayes and was considered the fastest shooter, a skill for which he had received a certificate at a prestigious military institution in the United States. When the car taking the son of Francois Duvalier, Jean-Claude, then a young kid, to school, was shot at and he almost got killed, Duvalier and his entourage decided the perpetrator must have been Francois Benoît, the son in law of the Edlines, the sharp shooter. Duvalier then sent his thugs after them who burned the house of the Benoîts to the ground including his parents and the servants, they kidnapped the 2 year old young daughter of Jacqueline Edline, then Francois' wife; the daughter disappeared forever and it is said she had been sacrificed in a voodoo ceremony. As for the Edline family, some got killed, some escaped. One of them was my age and used to be my playmate. Benoit and his wife and other members of the family took refuge at foreign embassies and were sent abroad.

Luckily, my sister was not there when the perpetrators came. On her way from the Faculté de Médecine, the medical school: "Stay away", said someone to her; "stay away", the macoutes are at the Edline's". She did but she could have been in the middle of it.

Later it was learned that the person who shot at Duvalier's son was Barbot, a former duvalierist, not Benoît.

My childhood times were thus dominated by the paranoia of Papa Doc whose competitors and enemies had regrouped abroad and launched several attempts at overthrowing him. Even within the military not all were considered loyal so seventeen officers were executed and the president took control of the army. Boats landed at several parts of the country carrying the rebels or in Creole 'kamoken' who wanted to overthrow the government. The repression was severe and there were a lot of political prisoners. Many were killed in the "vespers of Jérémie" when the mulattoes of that town were assassinated by the army officers and tontons macoutes after thirteen young men, most of them mulattoes, invaded the country by the port of Dame-Marie in the Grand-Anse region. Two of the thirteen young rebels were made prisoners and taken to a Port-au-Prince jail and they were executed in front of a large crowd of students, to set an example.

My father was right: in Haiti, one should stay away from politics if you could.

Duvalier installed a dictatorship and a dynasty through systematic repression. Opposition from left to right was crushed. Even the walls were considered to have "ears" so you couldn't critique his regime from the privacy of your home. Rebels and revolutionaries stopped invading the island by the sea in the hope of putting an end to his domination. Appalled and frightened, people stayed away. It was as they say in our country "the peace of the cemeteries".

17

7

My best buddies

And my best friend came to town. I must have been 8 or 9. She was the daughter of my mother's friend, so our mothers introduced us to each other. Her father, a judge, had been assigned to work at another part of the country; but he died, so the family of 7 children, 4 boys and three girls, returned to live in their native town, Aux Cayes.

She fulfilled a long yearning on my part for a best friend. She was my age and very smart; we disputed each other the head of the class. So we competed a little bit but it was okay: she wasn't my rival; she was my dearest friend, as intelligent as I was.

In and out of school we spent a lot of time together. We wrote each other letters, sharing all our little secrets and dreams. For a long time, I kept our correspondence, but finally lost the letters preserved in a plastic bag on my last stay in Haiti in my forties. In my mind, ours was a permanent bond, a mutual pact of love, fidelity and responsibility. Nobody could take me away from her so nobody would be able to take her away from me. I would not betray her and she would not betray me. I had no doubts her feelings for me were identical to my feelings for her. She came in my life when every one else failed me and bullied me, she comforted me, rescued me and stood by me and I would comfort her and stand by her forever. In her, I found a second self, we were a single soul dwelling in two bodies (Aristotle) and although we would grow separately we would never grow apart.

There were signs that showed we were developing independently; I refused to acknowledge them. First, her family's economic condition was more precarious than mine, her mother being a widow with seven children. This situation made them more vulnerable than we were. Second, I was a skinny girl slow to physically and psychologically mature, she was not and thus, early, attracted the attention of males. Third, she had an independent mind and grew to disagree with my views on several occasions.

My best friend faced early with the realities of life came out of her childhood earlier than I did. She did not have a responsibility to me; she had one to herself and her family, so our lives went their own path and destiny. Twice I influenced reality to be close to her, so we could have a similar fate, and protect our relationship; first by becoming her friend through my mother and two by going to the same Catholic school after we completed our primary school. But I did not have the power or the means to continually intervene when she was older. So we went our separate ways.

On my side too there were signs of separateness. I took piano and guitar lessons. I became the only young girl playing the guitar in town-although as a beginner. My family took the path of emigration. In effect, in the early sixties, my uncle Louis and my aunt Carmen went to Chicago and from there my aunt went to New York. It was the beginning of the Haitian middle class departure to a better life in the U.S.A. And from there they were able to help us financially and send for us. My girlfriend and her family emigrated to the Capital Port-au-Prince where she went to the public Lyceum while I went to a private secondary school.

But prior to that time, while we were still in Aux Cayes, and I was about 13-14, my beloved father became sick and he died when I was fifteen. He had tuberculosis and heart complications. It was for our family a very painful experience. My best friend did not show up at the funeral. Only a distant friend came. I did not understand why she could not have seen her presence was an absolute necessity in this time of grief. I remember walking to the cemetery and when we arrived there watching putting my father's coffin down the ground and swearing I would never forget him.

I was angry. I was angry at God who, in my view, did not keep his promise to protect my loved ones. He broke our pact. From now on I concluded I was alone on this earth, no God would come to my rescue. My sentiments for God were profoundly affected. It was a turning point in my life and my somewhat innocent childhood was gone.

After several years of relative inner peace during which I felt comforted especially by the love of my family and best friend and the presence of God, my happiness and tranquility were challenged again by these somber and traumatic events.

I had a special relationship with my father. Although silent and not demonstrative, our feelings for each other were profound. I don't ever remember my father saying to me: I love you or kissing me or hugging me or ever giving me presents or even holding my hand, but there was between us the sentiment of being secretly bonded, a sense of reciprocal recognition and appreciation as if we had signed a mutual pact of love.

Since I was a good student, he never had to punish me for poor school work or bad grades so our relationship was never fractured or challenged.

And so, I naturally developed a liking for boys my age.

*

I was on vacation and in the middle of a romance with an attractive adolescent who was finishing his secondary school at the prestigious St. Martial Seminary in Port-au-Prince, when we heard of my father's illness. He was soon to die, and me, my sisters and my brother returned to Les Cayes from Duvalierville to be there for him.

I felt so guilty. Having been brought up in the Catholic religion, I was already feeling so for having sexual desires, for being attracted to this young man although ours was a platonic relationship. Then,

I sensed I should have been there when my father died and not away having fun and being happy.

For a long while, I remained faithful to my father. Swearing I will never forget him, I held his memory inside of me. Long after I quit wearing black to pay my respects, he was there, filling me with grief and melancholy and the overwhelming idea of the inescapability of death.

So had vanished from my life my father, my best friend and God, my heavenly protector, all who kept me feeling secure and who allowed me to go through the necessary stages of life and developing into a healthy adolescent and adult. And, although I made friends again, I remained vulnerable and sensitive to the loss of loved ones... unable to pull myself together after heartbreaks and always yearning for steady, never-ending relationships.

8

Of Class and Color Prejudices

I have no recollections of my sister S as a young child and when I reached the age when memories are formed and preserved she had gone to the capital city, Port-au-Prince, to attend the teachers' college, *L'Ecole Normale d'Institutrices* so she could become an Elementary School teacher.

When she came back to town she was in age to work, get courted and then get married.

Her involvement with men gave rise to a lot of social awareness on my part, allowing me to get a feeling for both the class question and the color question in the provincial town.

At first, she was courted by a young man from the traditional Cayenne bourgeoisie. They were well established, respected mulattoes. Everybody was very happy with this relationship and my parents probably crossed their fingers it would lead to marriage. This relationship was short lived.

She was also solicited by a black middle class military officer. The army officers had a lot of prestige under former president Eugene Magloire and even under Francois Duvalier, especially at the beginning of his presidency. Despite the political twist to this relationship, it would have been also a good situation for her, I think. It did not last either.

Things started to take a bad turn, so to speak, when she became involved with a middle-class mulatto young man. He came from a socio-economically challenged single mom family. He was a handsome young man and my sister was in love with him.

The young couple was determined to stay together. So my parents accepted the *fait accompli* and supported them. They got engaged. He would visit his fiancée and they stayed in the living room downstairs hugging, kissing and touching each other.

The wedding was organized. The reception took place upstairs in our living room as the house was repaired and furbished for the circumstance. She wore a beautiful, long, white dress with hand made embroideries and there were at least ten flower girls all beautifully attired, some coming from the upper classes as well. My mother was the bridesmaid. It was a big wedding which took place at St Michael church on the outskirt of town.

The class and color question in Haiti goes back to colonial times. The colony had three social groups or castes: the whites, the affranchis composed mainly of mulattoes, and the slaves composed mainly of blacks. The affranchises were much more important in the south where I came from than in the north. Our town, thus, had more mulattoes. The affranchis, as the name indicates, had been freed from slavery and, in addition, had possessions: In 1789, they owned 2/3 of the land and ¼ of the slaves.

The conflict between André Rigaud, a southern mulatto born of a French nobleman and a black woman, and Toussaint Louverture, a northern black, is of particular interest. A champion of the rights of the free 'people of color', meaning the affranchis, André Rigaud's army established itself during the mid-1790s as a leading force in the South and was given authority to govern this region by the French.

Toussaint Louverture, however, was his superior in rank in the French Revolutionary Army of Saint-Domingue, then, Haiti's name. Rigaud refused to acknowledge the authority of the black revolutionary leader causing the bitter "war of the knives" as it was called. The two men fought over the control of Haiti after defeating foreign forces. They, later on, were both made prisoners by the

French who wanted to re-establish slavery on the island and were both imprisoned in Fort de Joux in the Jura Mountains in France.

History books report that Rigaud believed in a class system with mulattoes just below whites and blacks at the bottom. Toussaint, of course, would have none of this. To him mulattos and blacks were equal. In Rigaud's army, no blacks rose above the rank of captains. He was to return to Haiti with the Leclerc expedition on behalf of Napoleon; however he reunited with the army of Dessalines to proclaim Haiti an independent nation.

Later, he joined the forces which separated the South from the North and two of his protégés, the mulattoes Pétion and Boyer, became presidents of the South of Haiti.

The American occupation of Haiti during nineteen years (1915-1934) reinforced mulatto economic, political and social predominance. Haiti went back to Pétion and Boyer times where government was entirely staffed by the mulatto elite. There were Blacks in the government but not at the top. Social clubs tended to become limited to members of a particular group...

Under President Elie Lescot, the mulattoes had unchallenged political supremacy...

In 1946 a "revolution" took place where the blacks returned to high positions in the government when the two chambers elected Dumarsais Estimé as president of the republic. Estimé was the first black president in thirty years. "It is recognized by all that it was a peaceful and yet profound change: it was a social and nationalist explosion. The 30-year lid placed on the black middle class by the mulatto oligarchy had blown off. Overnight there rose to power members of the black lower, middle and upper class of Port-au-Prince and of the provinces" (Lyonel Paquin: The Haitians, Class and Color Politics).

From 1950 to 1956, Paul Eugène Magloire, a black colonel of the army, became president of Haiti. He understood the need for a 'balanced' government, between the mulatto and the black, Paquin writes.

I was born under president Estimé who was a black man and promoted blacks but I became aware of racial and social relations under President Duvalier when the war within the political class among mulattoes and blacks reached a culminating point. As time went by and the *noirist* ideology prevailed, color prejudice became less ostentatious and less obvious although the black political class delighted in courting and marrying light skin young women.

In fact I remember the economic elite composed of both mulattoes (the Bayard, the Bourgeois, the Blanchet, families) and blacks (the Pierre family) and the political elite equally composed of both mulattoes (Déjoie) and blacks (Edgar Néré Numa, René Condé, and Lesage Chéry). But color prejudice still prevailed.

Our family belonged to none of these "elitist" categories. We were modest people who distinguished ourselves by our intelligence and tried to build an acceptable life for ourselves through education. Too many of us in the family were women and despite the progress (right to vote, right to become medical doctors and so on), women were still oppressed. Besides, we refrained from relationships with people from the government who would exchange upward mobility for sexual favors, and kind of were prepared and expected to make it on our own.

In Aux Cayes, in fact, poor mulattoes married into the middle class black families to improve their social condition. Beauty was not exclusively related to the mulatto category neither was wealth. In 1960, the black beauty, Claudinette Fouchard, beat contestants from 42 other countries of the Caribbean and Latin America to win Haiti's Sugar Queen Title. She visited the town of Aux Cayes and I remember seeing her motorcade from the balcony of my house and being proud and filled with admiration. Later, when a mulatto woman from our town, Micheline Condé, won the title of Miss Haiti, she did not replace her in my heart. Everybody in Haiti was in awe with the black (or brown if you prefer) beauty queen. I, at least, felt that way.

At this time, social divisions, the question of class, were important especially when it came to getting seriously involved with the other sex and getting married. When a black young man from the Cayenne bourgeoisie courted me, one of my friends let me know bluntly he would never be allowed to marry because of the differences in our social conditions: "who is talking of marriage? I am just fifteen!" I answered her angrily.

The relationship did not last. Pat moved on leaving me with a broken heart.

Same thing for my oldest sister who as she went to medical school was courted by a couple of young men from the upper middle class who moved on when they realized our family wasn't wealthy. She eventually went on to marry a young man she had met at the Faculté de Médecine who was a student-doctor like her and whose father was a military officer under the government of Paul Eugène Magloire, the president who preceded Duvalier.

It was another big wedding this time even bigger at the capital city Port-au-Prince at the Christ the King church in the neighborhood of Bourdon.

9

In the fifties and sixties, it was pretty much an interconnected world...

World culture came to us and impacted us through various channels including radio, cinema, literature, and, in the capital city, for a few, television.

In Aux Cayes, my hometown, the southern Haiti Baptist church established Radio Lumière in 1959. I remember listening to classical music and the news on this radio station. It was the voice of the Protestant church in Haiti and probably an instrument of American influence, but I remained untouched by the politics as well as the rivalry between the Protestants and the Catholics. I was too young to be concerned with this serious business. My father had an old radio and there I learned of the assassination of President J.F. Kennedy which shocked everybody. I wasn't concerned with the politics. He was a head of state of international reputation who got shot abruptly. That's all you needed to be appalled and filled with sadness.

Through the radio stations broadcasting from Port-au-Prince, we heard the songs of Francoise Hardy, Sylvie Vartan, Johnny Halliday, Eddy Mitchell of the Ye-ye period. Charles Aznavour, Dalida and others charmed us through the air waves as well. The local music groups en vogue: Raoul Guillaume, Nemours Jean-Baptiste, Des Jeunes, Webert Sicot. In our town, Méridional and Panorama took the stage at the new movie theater. We also appreciated Latin American music especially coming from Cuba and Mexico. The Mexican woman singer Amalia Mendoza was a great star in Haiti and although our Spanish was rudimentary we all loved Daniel Santos, Celia Cruz, Edyie Gorme, danced the cha cha cha, and the bolero. We sang the rancheras and played the guitar with the group of local troubadours.

There was also the influence of Anglo-Saxon and Black American music: The Beatles were big in Haiti as well as Bob Dylan; we learned to dance the twist. We appreciated the music of Elvis Presley, Ray Charles and the Platters. The great Nat King Cole charmed our ears and delighted our emotions. And so on...

We were mostly mimicking the West but did not feel oppressed by Western culture. It had more to do with being part of the world, like adolescents go through similar experiences and feelings, dreams and pleasures. Besides, this participation to world culture did not assume a rejection of our own. We also enjoyed our local musical groups and folklore. At least I did.

There was jazz and instrumental music, too; especially by the black American Sydney Bechett, and the Italian Fausto Papetti. There was a true passion for music of different genres including classical music.

Movies were important as a form of entertainment and an influence on our ideas, values and lifestyle. Those shown at our local movie theater came from Europe especially France as well as the USA. The people from Aux Cayes were particular in their relationship to cinema. Once they loved a movie they wanted to see it over and over again. So such films as Marie Madeleine, the musical Seven Wives for Seven Brothers, The movie The Blue Angel, Carmen de Granada, the Ten Commandments, Cleopatra, the Count of Monte Cristo, Scheherazade, Sinbad the Sailor and others were shown over and over again.

During the mid- sixties more serious themes were introduced. In the U.S. and France, adolescents began to question traditional mores and wanted to imprint their own ideas and values on society. Times were changing. The movies began to show the moral hypocrisies in small U.S. towns as well as the sexual revolution that was happening. Love and sex were portrayed as natural psychological and biological phenomena that were oppressed in a society hung on false morality. We loved "Peyton Place" and the "Return of Peyton Place" which were adapted in French. I also had a special preference for the film "The Children's Place" played by Audrey Hepburn and Shirley Mc Lain addressing issues related to homosexuality. From Italy, we were getting great films with the stars Sophia Loren, Gina Lollobrigida, Claudia Cardinale and Marcello Mastroiani. The movie "Divorce, Italian Style" developed the themes of crumbling marriages, breakups, divorces and extra-marital affairs. Of course in those times, divorces were forbidden so the issues raised by the movie were of special interest. From France, we got Brigitte Bardot's movie "And God Created Women" which was explicit about sexuality and nudity. I was not allowed to see it because of my young age although I wanted to. I was eager to be exposed and participate to the new debate and options about sex and other philosophical and political ideas which put into question our society, traditions and mores and stimulated the intellectual discussion.

There were, despite the enormous differences in our societies, parallels with our small town life where a ban was placed on adolescent sexuality and scandals like abortion, illegitimate children, bigamy and adultery as well as premarital sex did occur. There was a definite shift from the lifestyle of the fifties as the adolescents of that period were getting ready to put forward their own ideas and viewpoints and claim the right to participate in the struggle for sexual liberation, feminism and against social divisions and racial oppression, thus affirming themselves as different from their elders.

And of course I was an avid reader. I recall among numerous others the volumes of Comtesse de Ségur's Les Malheurs de Sophie, Grimm's fairy tales Snow White, Beauty and the Beast, the Three Little Pigs... and the Book of One Thousand and One Nights in which imagination went wild with the stories of Ali Baba and the forty thieves, Scheherazade and Sinbad the Sailor. I remember being profoundly touched with Les Misérables of Victor Hugo recounting the life of Cozette at the Thénardiers.

I was also reading the books and magazines my brother brought home. That's how I became involved in the stories of Bleck le Roc, the hero who fought for the freedom of his country, America. They take place in the times prior to American independence when Great Britain considered North America as its property for commercial and military dominance. It is in this context that Bleck helps the fight and represents an ideal of liberty and resistance against the oppressor. As a people who promoted independence for all nations after we fought for ours and obtained it in 1804, we all identified with Bleck and waited impatiently for the next issue of Kiwi magazine.

I was very moved by St Exupéry' The Little Prince. This book became my favorite for the longest time. I still remember from it that idea: friendship is to create bonds, to be attached to somebody in a special manner...forever. That was the book that reflected an important theme and preoccupation of my childhood years.

And, much later, into my adolescence, I shed a lot of tears over the story of the princess of Cleves caught between her love and the prevailing morality of her time.

10

It's Time To Move On -1

At the age of fourteen, still in my prime adolescence, would I be able to turn my back away from my childhood ways and succeed in facing up to the challenges of my teen years?

It wouldn't be an easy task, for, as a child, the frail little girl I was had to fight epic battles against the bullies of my hometown with help from my best friend. I also had to face a high rank official of the government, a boogeyman, or *Tonton Macoute*, if you prefer, who wanted to deprive me of the affection of my friends, as well as the hypocrisy of the Catholic sisters of my secondary school who preferred the other kids.

My best friend, Nedje, was all I got outside of my family to fulfill my needs for attention, affection and companionship. And it was thanks to her that I was able to ignore the bullies and escape the fate of social isolation they had casted on me. With my best friend, I had an exclusive rapport and one wondered whether I would be able to develop more mature relations and survive our separation.

Early in my life, I had made mine those words of St Exupéry book The Little Prince:

- "Friendship is to create bonds, to be attached to somebody in a special manner…forever."

But Nedje had recently moved to the capital city, Port-au-Prince, toward a better life for her and her family and had left me alone to fend for myself. However, I was no longer a child. I had attained the age of fourteen and was stronger thanks to the love of my family and that of Nedje. So, I opened up to other, more mature relationships that would sustain my adolescent years.

*

I enjoyed spending my summertime out of town, in the countryside. It was usually at a nearby locality, close to the southern provincial town of Les Cayes where my parents were established and I was born.

The summer of 1963 would be spent differently in the locality recently renamed Duvalier Ville by the dictator Duvalier, who dreamed of building a modern town for the townsfolk of Cabaret, 24 kilometers north of the capital city, Port-au-Prince.

My sister, as a resident doctor in the town, lived in one of the newly built houses. There, she had a small room transformed in a medical clinic where she treated mostly cases of diarrhea in babies who did not have access to clean water and were dying of dehydration; there were also some instances of pregnant mothers giving birth, sometimes in the middle of the night. She had invited several members of the family over for the summer.

*

Ready or not you cannot remain a child. Life forces changes on you making you an adolescent and you have new tasks and developmental stages facing you. Whether or not you come to this time prepared depends upon the circumstances of your life and the help you had gotten.

At the age of fourteen, I had attained the time when my body significantly changed with my first period. Since nobody had prepared me for this eventuality to sexually develop, the advent of my first period was accepted with a lot of embarrassment and feelings of shame. It happened at Duvalier Ville while I was bathing and where for a terrifying moment I thought my blood was flooding the river.

Sexuality and sexual desire became more of a reality in my teen years but retained a repressed character due to the overall trends in the culture. Only a very small minority dared crossing the line and abortion was encountered with severe blame and reprobation. While in some cultures times had changed and the first sexual experience occurred in late adolescence, in Haiti, marriage continued to be enforced in the middle class as the turning point that would allow sexual intercourse to happen.

The prevailing moral viewpoint had the merit of protecting young adolescents from getting too involved sexually and having unwanted pregnancies which they were not prepared for and would have caused a scandal.

*

Mick was a handsome, articulate, and intelligent young man. He liked girls. He was a charmer and he charmed me. My sister, the resident-doctor, had organized a party for me on the occasion of my fifteenth birthday and that's how I met some of the young people who resided in the town of Duvalier Ville. Mick and I were attracted to each other as we danced together. It was a good feeling. He was attending one of the best Catholic schools of the country: the Saint Martial College in Port-au-Prince. That added a plus to his image. He had just passed his baccalaureate exams and must have been seventeen or eighteen. He whispered in my ears words that made me feel good as we danced in harmony.

We met on a few occasions and talked and were pleased with each other. At the Sunday ball, at the music of the northern "*Septentrional*" orchestra, we danced again and liked it.

Mick attracted me physically and intellectually. We decided to have a *rendez-vous* at the new modern cockfighting facility so we could be alone, touch, kiss and talk. But my older brother had followed me and asked me to go back home. It was humiliating, and unnecessary. I felt like a small child being scolded. How far could we go in the open space of the modern cockfighting facility? Why be so negative about adolescent sexuality? Why end what should have been one of my best moments to remember for all my life? These (sexual) feelings were good and positive and we should have been allowed to experience them. But the adults thought differently. For a while I resented my brother for having put an end to my escapade.

*

Mick was soon to go abroad to France to study. Although I had come back to my hometown and we were already separated, his departure and absence saddened me. And although we wrote letters to each other for a while, the relationship did not survive on the long term. As the adage says: *loin des yeux, loin du coeur...*

*

The difficulties I encountered as a child left me vulnerable but after a while it was time to leave behind my childhood and face the challenges and experiences of adolescence. It was time to form new relationships with both young girls and young boys that would nurture me and accompany me throughout my teenage years. I was no longer obsessed with the idea of having one best friend.

11

It's Time To Move On -2

After I completed my primary school, I wanted to be with my best friend at the private Catholic school. My mother supported my choice and I attended the secondary institution "Externat St Joseph" administered by the St Francis of Assisi sisters. There, I spent four years of my early adolescence, still stuck in my childhood ways for a while, competing with my friend for the head of the class and additionally for the affection of the sisters, still longing for exclusive rapport and hungry for attention.

The St Francis of Assisi sisters did not have the capacity to prepare the students for the classes and public examinations that marked the completion of secondary school, and so I spent a year at the public lyceum "Philippe Guerrier" in the company for the first time of students of the opposite sex.

But prior to that, friendship came more easily to me than it did during my childhood since I developed a closer relationship with several of my classmates at the Sisters' school. At the Lyceum I also developed friendship ties with some of the young men; the young males who attended the lyceum and my male professors had a different, more positive appreciation of me. It was a more relaxed situation not as intense as the friendship I experienced during my childhood.

After my father died, my mother was able to financially provide for my education thanks to his pension funds, so I did not stay at the public lyceum. She paid for me to attend the prestigious Centre d'Etudes Secondaires in Port-au-Prince where instruction was presented by such famous professors as Pierre Riché, professor of Mathematics, Pradel Pompilus, professor of Literature, and Jean Claude, professor of Philosophy who had degrees from France. We also had Apollon and Zamor as professors of Haitian history and others.

At the Centre d'Etudes, I had two girlfriends too whom I invited for a stay with me at Aux Cayes at my aunt's for my mother had already traveled to New York where she emigrated.

I did not like the fact that my mother had left. From my own point of view, I was unable to see the departure of our parents, sisters, brothers, aunts, to be the natural order of things. We love and are attached to our country of birth and should remain in it to have our life and contribute. This idea of preparing human resources that would constitute the workforce in foreign countries did not appeal to me. But it was the direction our society was going to. Many families traveled to the newly liberated countries of Africa too and so did my half brother. By the time I was sixteen or seventeen seven of us had traveled abroad to make a living and/or study including him. There was nothing I could do about it. Besides, there were no jobs and my mother's commerce was no longer viable. I too would have soon to pack and leave to pursue post-secondary studies at the University and work to make a living for myself.

M. shared his music with me. He lent me four of his records, among them Charles Aznavour's, which I took with me to Aux Cayes where I went back after the vacation ended. I listened to them and remembered him. We wrote each other letters. But he was soon to go abroad to France to study. His departure and absence saddened me. Until I let go and met P., a young man from my hometown.

Like my sisters and brothers before me, I had moved to the capital, Port-au-Prince, to complete my secondary studies. At the Centre d'Etudes Secondaires, it was a successful adaptation both academically and socially. Of course the students there had advantage and predominance as compared to those who came from the provinces: they were more advanced intellectually and socially more emancipated. They had come of age and were no longer held back in their childhood.

Coming from the St Francis of Assisi sisters and the public lyceum of a provincial town, I managed however to retain a good academic position and standing: although no longer the sole head of the class, I was among the first five and positively regarded by the professors. My friendship with three of the girls was a more casual relationship and not an emotional, exclusive attachment. More of an adult like type of bonding. They were my study bodies and my companions outside of school.

I had successfully moved on with my life.

12

In Search of Eternal Love

In 1964, our country was the theater of many events that were to change Haitian society and its people forever.

Papa Doc's regime which had already established its brutal and repressive character since he created his civil militia known as the "*Tontons Macoutes*" was taking a turn for an even worse course. His presidency became a self-proclaimed dictatorship when he dissolved the parliament, amended the constitution and declared himself president for life.

To mark this significant shift, (his "revolution" as Duvalier conceived it), the black and red flag of Jean-Jacques Dessalines was restored, the currently adopted blue and red flag was changed to being vertically divided and the Phrygian liberty cap above the palm tree was removed. Duvalier put a guinea hen in the middle of the flag.

That year, during the summer, thirteen young men (mostly mulattoes) arrived on the shores of Dame-Marie in the Grand Anse Department (South Coast) to launch a guerilla movement aimed at putting an end to the repression and the abuses of power perpetrated by the government. In their view, the people of the South, where they came from, would stand in solidarity and accompany them in their quest to crush the dictatorship. What they found instead were the civil militia and army battalions that were infiltrated in the provinces and the localities and whose reaction was criminally repressive.

The thirteen young men were captured one by one and they were beheaded except for two: Numa and Drouin were taken to Port-au-Prince and imprisoned. The dictator then ordered a "public execution" of the two "guerilleros" near the public cemetery in Port-au-Prince, attended by delegations of school children. In retaliation, Duvalier's secret police also slaughtered whole families, especially from the southern town of Jérémie where these young men mostly originated.

I remember. I was on a visit to a locality on the southern coast when these events occurred, since I enjoyed going to the countryside during the summer time, and I have the memory of being filled with disgust and a sense of reprobation at the cruel conduct and actions by the *macoutes*.

We lived in a country where Duvalier's ideology was dominating all aspects of life including by his reference to voodoo and superstition as a means to extend his power over the masses. He even claimed president Kennedy's assassination in 1963 was the result of a curse he placed on him. His voodoo powers thus were extended, in his propaganda, beyond Haiti's borders.

While aid was suspended under pressure from the Kennedy government due to the evidence of corruption, it was gradually reinstated after the death of the U.S. President and the view of Haiti as "an essential bulwark" in the fight against communism in the Caribbean and Latin America, prevailed.

Haiti was favored as a place to receive immigrants by the U.S. and our educated middle-class was depleted in favor of Chicago, New York and Montreal.

From my own point of view, I was unable to see the departure of our parents, sisters, brothers, aunts, cousins, to be the natural order of things. We love and are attached to our country of birth and should remain in it to have our life and contribute. This idea of preparing human resources that would constitute the workforce in foreign countries did not appeal to me. But it was the direction our society was going to. Many families were travelling to the newly liberated countries of Africa too, to contribute to the new black education force, and so did my half brother.

By the time I was eighteen, seven of us had traveled abroad to make a living and/or study including him. There was nothing I could do about it. Besides, there were no jobs and my mother's commerce was no longer viable. So she left. I too would have soon to pack and leave to pursue post-secondary studies at the University and work to make a living for myself.

In fact, the middle class who had begun to emerge in greater numbers since the governments of Dumarsais Estimé and Paul-Eugène Magloire saw its social and economic conditions deteriorating. It could not survive thanks to small commerce or teaching jobs or being a low-level government employee or a seamstress. There were no employment opportunities for the youth who came out of school. Only in the bourgeoisie could someone earn money through commerce or business and, of course, high-level government officials and their connections were also able to make a living for themselves and their families.

In our southern town there were two migration movements: of those who left to go to the capital, Port-au-Prince, either to study or work; and, of those who left to go abroad for the same purposes.

As young adolescents who could not influence history on a large scale, we, therefore, went with the flow while trying to have our small impact on society. It is within this context that we had to live our lives going through teen experiences and coming of age in a difficult period in a country going through fundamental changes while we ourselves were developing.

(2)

I don't recall exactly where I met Pat, but it must have been on the upper side of town where the richer and the more privileged had their homes.

He was indeed a young, tall male, about 3 years older than I was, and he came from a family who resided in a solid, elevated building that was hidden from public view by a large and long garden. His family possessed thousands of acres of land in the region of Les Cayes, near Camp-Perrin, where it had a second home for the summertime. They owned two money-making stores where they sold imported goods. They also exported the "vetiver" grass which was used abroad to make expensive perfume. And, they had industrial facilities. They probably had other sources of wealth I was not aware of like money in the bank, investments abroad, etc…

Pat's uncle was an agronomist, having studied at a prestigious university in Europe at a time when only the rich could study abroad. They were one of the few families who possessed a car in aux Cayes. Some of them were well traveled, having been to Europe and the United States at a time when middle class Haitians had no idea what Paris, London, Brussels or New York looked like.

In fact, I was introduced to Pat through my friend Manou whom I met at the Catholic sisters' school. At the age of fifteen, friendship came more easily to me than it did in my childhood. I made friends both among young girls and young boys and I had forgotten about the bullies of my childhood. Later, I realized my friend Manou was secretly in love with Pat but he chose me to be his girlfriend and she became jealous of our relationship. On one occasion, she bitterly and bluntly told me:

-   "His family will never allow him to marry you".
-   "Who is talking of marriage?" I answered emotionally. "I am just fifteen!"

What Manou was referring to though is the reality that Pat and I did not belong to the same social class and we did not seem to take that into account. I am from what Haitians refer as coming from the "classes moyennes" (middle class) my father being an administrator for the public schools and my mother holding a struggling commerce – although I understand it was successful in times past. As my mother says eloquently: "we were not rich, we were not poor" and although my family owned a house, was able to procure us with basic food and clothing, send some of us to the best private schools in town and then to the capital city, Port-au-Prince, there were people who had more means, were wealthier than us. We did not live in the same neighborhood nor go to the same church and it was through a lot of efforts and sacrifices that we went to the same schools. Ours was the Sacred Heart church across from the open market; theirs was the Cathedral across from the public square on the upper side of town. We lived in wood houses; they lived in concrete houses that were bigger. My mother had a struggling commerce; they had big stores and businesses. They sold fabric or imported shoes and other goods, exported coffee, plants and other agricultural products.

I remember Pat to be a tall and verbal young black man although not very successful in school. Pat was a confident young man who liked to show-off a bit. Several times, he passed my house driving his car up and down the street, so demonstrating his interest in having me as his girlfriend. Since few people owned a car in town, everybody on the block was impressed.

He was aware of our socio-economic differences but didn't seem to care. That gave him an advantage and added to his personality as I saw it. We were young and untouched by the idea that social differences could be an obstacle among people who liked each other. Besides, we were living in the moment and although we were sincere in our feelings did not envision serious matters like getting married where the opinion of our parents would matter.

I let go of my fears and guard and became attached to him. Pat's affection reassured me and comforted me. He was like a substitute for my father although he was not a father figure. I still held the idea that you were to be loved by someone special in your life so you could go on. He filled this need for love and also made me feel good about myself. In my mind, our relationship was not a fling or a flirt, something of no consequence. Pat would always be there for me and I could count on him for being a special friend. Later, when we would be older, we would have a more mature, adult type relationship. In the meantime, we held hands, danced at balls and kissed hastily. And that was enough for me. Was it for him?

I was about to turn sixteen and my father had died when I was fifteen. It was a severe blow to my emotional development.

With my father's passing, I had suffered the loss of someone who loved me dearly and whose unconditional affection I relied on in order to grow and engage in more mature relationships. His death was a turning point in my life.

My best friend had left our hometown with her family for a better life in Port-au-Prince. My mother had followed my aunts and some of my siblings to New York; and my belief in God as my heavenly protector was fractured due to the premature death of my father. As a child, I loved God with all my heart. However, my commitment to God was conditional: he was all powerful and would take me under his wings, secure me from harm and the death on my loved ones. I was a fragile child who needed to feel safe and that's the way I could figure out my relationship to God. He was my protector in heaven. In return, I would be a good girl and would commit no sin.

Pat came into my life at this specific juncture where all – or almost all - my love supports were gone. I trusted him to feel the void. That was probably too much to ask of an adolescent male who was looking forward to grow normally, have flings, flirts and fun.

(3)

As for Pat, he continued to visit me from time to time. He too had arrived in Port-au-Prince to continue his studies and resided in wealthier Pétion Ville while I lived on board in the upper middle-class neighborhood of Bourdon.

My father had died the year before and I was still grieving his passing. For a time I was wearing black clothes as a sign of grief and respect and to show that his memory was still alive. I was shy, melancholic, sexually repressed and reserved, suffering from a regression in my emotional development and holding on unrealistic expectations as far as this relationship was concerned. After all, we did not have much in common. We belonged to two different worlds and did not have much to talk about when we were together.

When he let go of me I wasn't ready. I was in disarray. But, after a while, I understood and accepted that Pat, who visited me to reassure me of his affection, had to move on and meet girls who had more to offer.

After I clung on to him for a while, I accepted that Pat and I had to go our separate, "independent" ways. I left behind the unrealistic attachment to him and the trauma of our separation and faced life standing alone as I was assured of his distant affection and of that of my family and friends.

And this chapter of my life underwent a closure. After all, a young adult in order to develop and enter more mature relationships that would eventually lead to engagement and marriage must be able to go beyond childhood ways of relating as well as adolescent crushes based on affective needs and unrealistic expectations. My wound healed, and I became whole again – although still aspiring to love and be loved by someone forever some day.

13

Le Départ

Haiti is a land of emigration. This displacement of our workforce did not start recently. Eager to earn a living, our population has, since the 1930s, taken the road to exile leaving behind, but hoping to return to some day, its native country to which it has remained attached.

1

First, the Haitians went to Cuba where they worked as agricultural workers especially on the cane plantations.

"Haitiano maldito, negro de mierda", that is how they were called, while they toiled in the fields to help the Cuban economy. It is Jacques Roumain, the famous Haitian writer, who reminded us in his book "Masters of the Dew" while making of a Haitian peasant immigrant from Cuba he called Manuel the hero of his famous novel. Upon his return to his country, Manuel Jean-Joseph was going to reunite the divided community of Fonds-Rouge and there, he formed the "coumbite" to find the spring and the water to irrigate the arid land of his village.

Today, the descendants of these rural workers have integrated Cuban society where they have - I guess – participated in the socialist revolution to oust dictator Batista and establish a revolutionary regime.

If emigration and exile are fundamental themes of our lives and our literature, returning home is no less legendary, a desire which in some cases becomes reality.

2

There are Haitians immigrants who went to the Dominican Republic. At the time, it was - and it still is - mainly to work as cane cutters, though they have known better and more dignified days in the 19th century under the government of Jean-Pierre Boyer who proceeded to the reunification of the island, which was already the case under the administration of Toussaint Louverture in 1802.

One knows, at least by hearsay, the famous "*bateys*" or dwelling places of these workers of the cane plantations where our rural proletarians live in abject poverty conditions. More recently, in the Dominican Republic, our construction workers have contributed significantly to transform the neighboring country into modern cities. In addition, many of our children are begging on the streets of major cities and our merchants, on the frontier markets, are selling few agricultural products, an insignificant contribution of Haitian exports to a country that we enrich considerably with our imports.

In the forties, the Dominican dictator Trujillo proceeded to massacre a large number of our countrymen and our government then received little compensation in return for the damage done to our people.

Today we're talking about close to a half-million Haitians in our neighboring country where to the *braceros* were added several thousand students and other Haitian immigrants of all stripes.

3

Florida is the favorite destination of our "boat people", as they are called, and of many privileged Haitian students. Many members of our middle class and of the entrepreneurial class live there too.

We call the boat people "political refugees" rather than "economic refugees" thereby stressing that politics in Haiti is very important and determines the destiny of our people.

These come mainly from the north-west of Haiti and also from the Bahamas who themselves also have their "quota" of Haitians, some who are from time to time returned because living illegally in these countries, that is to say without a required immigrant visa.

4

Canada, the Province of Quebec first saw an influx of our intellectuals and professionals as well as our students and then accepted Haitians from more modest backgrounds. We have contributed to the development of this country as well as its share of taxi drivers and factory workers. More recently, Canada has requested sending Haitians to develop remote areas of this beautiful part of the world.

5

When I was in Paris in the late sixties and early seventies, there were mostly Haitian students living in France. The sons and daughters of the privileged, and, in lesser cases of middle-class parents, they came there - disdaining the Haitian University - for college and graduate study. Some of them were political exiles. They would go back home, after they graduated, or join another land of immigration like the U.S. and Canada, where they found work.

Today, there is a population of humble origin in France, including Paris. Passing through French Guyana, the Haitians have been able to visit the City of Lights and live there as immigrant workers.

6

As far as I know, in my family, it all started with my maternal grandmother named Litéla. They called her so, my mother told me, because being born a few months after her brother Ravil, everybody agreed: she was or had been there, in Creole Li te La and that she and Ravil were in fact twins.

A market merchant, she went to Cuba to get supplies for her display. My grandmother named Litéla was from St Jean du Sud, a locality which is, as its name suggests, on our southern coast. Turn left at Carrefour Joute on the way to the well-known beach Port Salut.

As a young adult, she found herself in Cavaillon, which is situated a few kilometers away from the entrance of Les Cayes. There she met my grandfather, Lamartinière, a teacher by profession, who was living with a woman of whom he had many children.

My grandparents settled in Cavaillon and therefore, as a child, I remember my Granny had a stall in the market, not far from the bridge over the river of the same name, famous for its crocodiles and its overflows. They had many children, including my mother, and went to reside in the town of Les Cayes, the capital of the Southern Department.

7

The first of her children to go abroad to stay was my uncle Lamarre, the eldest of the family. He was not yet married and had four daughters by his common wife. I was too young to remember him. He probably lived in precarious conditions and chose to leave for the city of Chicago, North America, to greener pastures. There he met a nurse from Port-au-Prince, who became his wife.

Then, my aunts Carmen and Agnes followed. My aunt Carmen was a nurse and Aunt Agnes was in the business of hand embroidery: tablecloths, wedding dresses, layettes, etc. They were to join my uncle Lamarre in Chicago where they found better pay for their work.

It is thanks to Aunt Carmen that we are here in North America because she worked with patience, determination and zeal to make us travel to the United States one after the other. She managed with the help of her lawyers to get us the affidavits of support, submitted her bank accounts and letters of invitation to the immigration authorities...

She did so well that my mother also left her native land, after the death of my father, and her business in decline, to go to New York. She joined her sisters Carmen and Agnes and five of us, my sisters and my brother, who had preceded her, leaving me with my younger sister behind with the plan to send for us later.

I had completed my high school studies and I was staying with relatives in my hometown, waiting there to join my family in Montreal. Indeed, there were my sister, a doctor, who had studied at the Faculty of Medicine of Port-au-Prince and my brother, a student in Biochemistry, who had successfully completed his secondary school with the Brothers of St. Louis de Gonzague. My plan was to apply at the University of Montreal where I wanted to study psychology and philosophy. I finally joined them in 1969 and from there went to Paris to study at the Sorbonne.

My Aunts Ava and Livia, my uncle Ted and their children came to New York much later, in the seventies and eighties. So much so that nobody in my family - except for my brother, on my father's side who had chosen the path of Africa in the mid-sixties and also my sister on my father's side - had remained in Haiti.

My aunt Ava was in Haiti a great seamstress. Her husband, one of the few partisans of Duvalier in the city of Les Cayes was assassinated by political rivals during the presidential campaign of 1956-1957. She found herself alone with her seven children. She joined my aunt's apartment in New York at 1548 President Street in Crown Heights, in the seventies.

My sister on my father's side, Flora, after working as a preschool teacher on the south coast near Port-Salut, had come to live in our family home in Les Cayes on Sténio Vincent Street. There, she opened a commerce and it is through this activity she could, she and her husband, educate their children so much so that her daughter who is very intelligent and studious as did my older sister attended the School of Medicine and her brothers studied at a private college to become engineers. Their father was a headmaster in the region of Les Cayes. He had been a member of Duvalier's militia wearing the occasional blue jean suit as required by the dictator.

8

My uncle Ted was a driver by profession. He was driving a van that belonged to him. He lived by the archdiocese of Les Cayes, at the entrance of *Nan Savann*, near the Ocean. He had a love marriage in defiance of social barriers. The couple had many children. He, too, his wife and their children found themselves in North America in the eighties where they settled.

9

Our family took root abroad, in North America, when its members found friends and spouses, some of them foreigners. They went to College and some to Graduate school. My mother now a hundred years old, has grand children and great grand children. In short, for my family, it was for most a successful integration and adaptation.

I would like to insert a few considerations about my aunt Livia who, a bit late in her life, had married one of the sons of a Protestant family of Les Cayes. Theirs was a large family. Her husband was special. He was one of the gentlemen who acted as "intellectuals", discussing politics and other topics when their group met in the restaurant/bar La Glacière drinking rum and whiskey. When I finished my Philosophy class, he took me one evening with him two friends I had invited to spend a holiday in my hometown, and I found myself a glass of rum in hand, chatting with his friends, comparing former president Soulouque regime to that of Francois Duvalier and the "Tonton Macoutes" to the "Zinglins."

Aunt Livia was an educator. She had friends from the Cayenne privileged elite. She and Tonton owned a house near the police station of Les Cayes. They had two children who went to Florida. When she had her visa that allowed her to travel, she did not settle in foreign land.

My brother and my sister on the paternal side have both passed away in their sixties. Their children have also taken the road to foreign land and live presently in New York and Boston. The latest addition is my brother's son who, after the earthquake of January 12,

2010 which killed 300.000, only dreamed of leaving Haiti. Having studied medicine at Notre Dame University in Port-au-Prince, he wants to pass the test that will allow him to work as a doctor in New York. As for my niece, also a graduate of the Faculty of Medicine of Port-au-Prince, she was finally able to successfully pass the test but has trouble finding employment. Other times, other manners, the quality of our medical school has dropped significantly and our doctors are no longer recognized and sought after as they were in the sixties and seventies.

10

I almost forgot to mention on my father's side my Aunt *Aurora* and her children, and grandchildren. And yet, except for my sister Flora, they are the ones I found in Les Cayes, when coming back from my big trip to America, I returned to my country to work, live and contribute.

14

These were Glorious Times

There was something magical or unexplainable about the way Glorious and I became friends, for, before that day, we never made eye contact and refrained from saying hi to each other even though we found ourselves face to face on the same sidewalk many times.

This day that we finally got acquainted, I was standing in front of a building with apartments for rent on Barclay Avenue near Parsons Boulevard in Flushing, Queens, when an invisible but insisting force propelled me toward her passing by. I stepped forward and said:

"Hello! My name is Maryse."

She answered:

"My name is Glorious. I live on the 3rd floor of your mom's building. I met you many times before but we never introduced ourselves."

I went to visit her one-bedroom apartment in my mom's building. It was uncluttered, clean and orderly with a piano. There were two large windows in the living room facing the sofa and letting in plenty of sunlight for the plants.

"I have been living here for five years", she said.

"My mother has been here for the last twenty-five years. Her apartment had become neglected by the landlord and she was tired of Brooklyn anyway. So, she and my sister moved to Flushing and now I live in Flushing too since I returned from Haiti" I told her.

Glorious and I planned going out together to bring some distraction and amusement to our dull and lonely lives.

I took her to the Queens Conservatory of Music, on Main Street, five blocks away, where there was a classical music recital by the students for free. She wasn't difficult and she loved music, being a blues singer herself, so she had a good time. We then went to my apartment on Ash Avenue, near Kissena Boulevard, and we ate tacos filled with spiced ground beef with lettuce and sour cream. I made her a glass of iced green tea to drink.

The next Saturday, after I came back from my job at the Flushing Public Library, we went again to the Conservatory of Music where the Moon Pool Jazz played United Funk and Swing.

I wonder where Glorious was on the 4th of July that year. I had nobody to go with to look at the fireworks in Astoria by the Hudson River near the Queensboro Bridge. My girlfriend Kate had taken some other friends and left me behind.

When there was a fire in my building in the month of June, I spent three nights at my friend Glorious' apartment and expected to spend many more while looking for a new place; but on the fourth night, while waiting for her phone call, I went to my mother's.

"Will she or won't she call", I said to myself. "I spent three nights at her place already. May be she won't be able to help me anymore. She is a Buddhist and believes in karma. May be she is superstitious and thinks bad luck is contagious. May be she feels she has done enough to help me."

Spending the night in my smoke-filled apartment on Ash Avenue is not a true alternative because I will not close my eyes for the night, after I have been so afraid of the fire. Like the other day, when I counted every hour while listening to the radio: the news on International France Radio and the BBC, jazz on Columbia University radio station and WBGO, and classical music on the New York Times station. And that's how I spent my night with my eyes wide open 'til morning.

It was 8:30 p.m. "She won't call", I said to myself. I have no place to spend the night but I don't want to call her myself. I found a new apartment but it will be available in eighteen days. Where will I sleep in the meantime?

But she finally does call me.

At her place that night, we watched her tape of Dorothy Donovan interpreting on piano "What Will you do the Rest of your Life" and we listened to two different versions of Duke Ellington's Take the A Train by Dorothy Donovan and the Three Mo' Tenors.

We ate salmon cakes that she made and grilled chicken.

We talked about slavery. It still hurts her like a fresh wound; In spite of all the time gone by.

Glorious and I made plans to go listen to music when we could make it. I took her to the theater at La Guardia Community College in Long Island City, and the Jamaica Arts Center in Jamaica, Queens. She took me to a concert at the Flushing Town Hall.

The concert was entitled: Jazz Live, A Night of Elegance, animated by the Jazz vocalist, Jon Hendricks, the Father of "Vocalese", or the art of setting lyrics to recorded jazz instrumental standards (such as the big band arrangements of Duke Ellington and Count Basie).

I was greatly entertained by the music of the lyricist Jon Hendricks who even mentioned our legendary heroes Toussaint Louverture and Dessalines while singing a Caribbean tune. Glorious had made a good choice.

Soon after, she was to move to a new apartment out of town and disappeared from my life leaving me with no one to accompany me to those jazz concerts.

It's difficult to make friends in Flushing Glorious, unless an invisible force comes into play to help forge our destiny. *Au revoir, mon amie.*

15

The Page

Chapter I

I had been looking for work without success for quite a while so I was particularly euphoric when I got hired at the Flushing Public Library as a page.

The library used to be a cramped place on Main Street by Northern Boulevard, however, since the Chinese and Koreans moved into the neighborhood some twenty years ago, a new three-story building was built at the junction of Kissena Boulevard and Main Street. I was to work in the basement by the auditorium in the section dedicated to adults learning English as a second language.

In fact, as was explained to me, I was to fix the books on the shelves, attend to the clients who came to the library, and last but not least, take the elevator to bring the returned books to the first floor.

I needed the job so I refrained from saying I was afraid of enclosed spaces and could not take the elevator by myself.

As Mara, the boss, explained to me I was to work seventeen hours a week earning 6 dollars an hour. My salary would thus be close to one hundred dollars a week. I was already dreaming about what I'd do with the money. Change the kitchen tiles which were in bad shape, buy new curtains (I did not have any), a bed (I only had a mattress and a box) and living room furniture. But first and foremost, I was to pay my debt which amounted to 6000 dollars. May be I would even be able to buy myself summer clothes and a pair of sandals...

Chapter II

At my work, at the library located three blocks away from my one-bedroom apartment on Ash Avenue, I met Jessica, the Chinese boss; Christina, the Haitian student; and Da Sin, the Chinese employee. There were two others: a Korean woman and a Porto Rican young lady whose names I did not know yet.

It's not hard work. And since I love to read and write, I imagined I could take a book on one of the shelves and read a little bit in my spare time. I was in familiar territory since it was the Center for Second Language Learning and I wrote my doctoral dissertation on the cognitive and language development of Haitian children.

Chapter III

While all the attendees are busy on their computer learning English, I read a bit.

Did you know the Taj Mahal, one of the world's wonders, situated in the northern part of India, takes its name after that of an Indian leader's wife? She was the "Pride of the Palace" and when she died, her husband ordered to make it her tomb. The works began in 1632 and it took the 20,000 workers more than 20 years to complete it.

Chapter IV

It's been a month and a half since I have been working at the library but I had not have yet the opportunity to go to the third floor, at the International Resource Center, to look at their French and Haitian collection.

They had no books on Haiti, except for Edwidge Danticat in the Literature section.

I visited their French collection finally. I borrowed a biography of the writer from Martinique, Aimé Césaire, written by Georges Ngal who is a novelist and literary critic. Césaire has written a book about Toussaint Louverture and one about Henri Christophe, who led our independence struggle against the French colonialists. He also wrote the famous *Cahier du Retour au Pays Natal* and *Et les Chiens se Taisaient*. As a writer, he is considered to be a member of the Negritude movement and of the Surrealist school. His writing is rhythmic like jazz and the African tam tam, Ngal writes. He has been influenced by Rimbaud and Lautréamont but also by Aragon, Breton...

However, «the main inspiration of Césaire remains the collective experience of the black man in time and space, (in history and Diaspora)...the condition of the black man from Martinique, the lynching in the Mississippi, and the pursuit of future slaves in the African forest...»I speak of millions of human beings», Césaire writes, «who learned to develop fear, a complex of inferiority and a sense of despair.»

Senghor, Césaire, Damas, Price-Mars, Jacques Roumain, Langston Hughes...These were great times for literature. But are we condemned to write about the suffering of the black man and his struggle to be free?

Chapter V

At the Flushing Public Library where I worked this summer, I met Louie, Lisa and Christina. They are young persons who fit better the definition of a page, having everything to learn in order to acquire work experience. Louie and Lisa have not finished their secondary school and Christina just completed her first year of college. As for the Chinese woman Da Sin and the Korean Sung Sook, I can barely understand what they are telling, their English being strongly accented and so is mine although a bit less. But I feel I am in good company. They are all very nice people. After having, for the longest time, wanted to do anything or almost rather than staying at home, I do not complain and until today have never missed a day of work or been late.

Chapter VI

I invited my co-workers from the library to an exhibit of paintings by my daughter's father-in-law in Manhattan. We were a small group of people including some Haitians and Haitian-Americans, friends of my daughter and of my son-in-law. We commented the paintings, drank some good wine and ate some cheese and crackers. None of my co-workers showed up. I figured they were not interested or curious.

My sister came by to have lunch with me by the library. I love the *crabs with ginger and scallions* from the nearby Chinese restaurant. I promised I would take her to Queensborough Community College to see an exhibit of African Art and to the Flushing Town Hall or else to the Voelker Orth house on 38th Street by my mother's house.

I read about the Flushing Town Hall. An old Town Hall, as the name indicates, it is now a house dedicated to the arts. The Flushing Council on Culture and the Arts operates it on behalf of the City of New York.

Jazz is an important component of art activities at the Flushing Town Hall as well as Latin American arts. The institution is known for its commitment to the jazz legacy.

Flushing, in fact, has been unique in hosting religious and ethnic minorities in New York. It is the first town in the Americas to guarantee religious freedom to all its citizens when the authorities of the 17th century demanded that "Quakers, Papists, Jews and other heretics be expelled." There was a reaction in the Flushing community when 30 petitioners wrote a letter in 1657 known as the Flushing Remonstrance to request and demand that freedom of religion be granted to these residents.

In the 19th century, Flushing became one of the centers of the abolitionist movement and was a major stop on the Underground Railroad to free the slaves.

Flushing population grew to include thousand of European immigrants and African American artists settled there as well, as they migrated from the south. In the 1970s, East Asian immigrants began to settle in Flushing where they now comprise 35% of the population.

When every client is busy listening to their cassettes or watching their videos, I read the correspondence of Georges Sand and Gustave Flaubert, two writers who loved writing with passion. I retain this passage by Flaubert when he was not working: "my inaction eats me like a cancer and I suffer horribly".

Chapter VII

Mara, the boss, did not like my reading activities. And, above all, I was not taking the elevator to bring back to returned books to the first floor.

So I got fired from my job.

16

Remembering Kate

Some twenty years since my mother left Brooklyn and moved to Queens, but I never met Kate in the building.

And yet, she had been living there with her mother for many years prior to renting her own studio at wealthier Jamaica Estates.

I met Kate's mother first—we shared an interest in Haiti's political drama—and later she introduced me to her daughter.

We became instant friends, Kate and I, sharing the love for good food, exotic music and endless conversations. She took me to restaurants and movie theaters, and I took her to jazz concerts at the College nearby. Listening to Michael Bublé on the car radio, we often traveled through East Village, stopping at a Thai restaurant to degust Thai beers. Michael Bublé… Good stuff. Kate has refined musical taste.

On the 4th of July last year, after the fireworks display in Astoria, by the Hudson River, we went for a long ride in her car on the highways of Long Island, listening to Brazilian jazz, flamenco and afro-Cuban compositions. No fixed destination. We ended up on Jones Beach, where we ordered grilled tuna, sautéed vegetables, and some bass at a small restaurant. While the local rock group played noisy and ragged music, I had a glass of wine, she had a beer. As usual, she paid the bill.

I could never afford to pay my friend Kate a meal, a movie ticket or a jazz concert. Those were economically-challenged times for me—no money for leisure activities.

I promised her a dinner at my house.

"What do you say? A tasty paella with lots of shrimps and mussels, an avocado salad, a mango for dessert…"

"And Sangria!" she exclaimed. "Don't forget the Sangria."

"We'll listen to Alicia Keys on my small stereo."

On Jones Beach that night, we talked about Saving Face, a movie adaptation of a novel by a Chinese woman who happened to live in Flushing, Queens. Kate said she knew about the movie; the plot revolved around a Flushing family facing a double taboo: the mother pregnant outside of marriage, the daughter a lesbian. A shadow passed over Kate as she spoke, and I wondered for a second whether Alice Wu, the Chinese woman author and movie director, knew Kate and her mother.

For this was their story.

After dinner, Kate gave me a book titled "Small Miracles of Love and Friendship." She'd marked her favorite passage: *Like magnets we are drawn to people and places that will complete us in some special way.* And this was true for Kate and me.

I asked her when I would see her again.

"*Tu as tes démons et moi les miens,*" she answered. You have your demons and I have mine.

She was right, I guess. Despite all that we shared—our interest in good music as well as movies and food…, our desire for endless, aimless rides, as well as conversations about Haiti (our native country) and the United States (our adopted country)—we each had preoccupations and needs that separated us irreparably. I didn't know of her battles. She didn't know of mine.

Kate is gone now; gone from my life.

Her mother says Kate is angry at me. Is it because I didn't visit her after the minor car accident? Have I e-mailed her the wrong lesbian joke?

I don't know.

For weeks now, I've been trying to make amends for an unknown fault, leaving messages on her answering machine.

Kate might be gone forever, and I have no other friend but her.

Kate, je me souviens.